AF482511

A word to the readers

Human today has fallen into a terrible fire, which is called Alienation. Self-forgetfulness causes human to give up loving himself and not discover a reason for his existence. When he cannot discover the cause of his own existence, at certain moments he engages in actions that are often unintentionally anti-human. He does not know what action he is taking and he does not know whether this action was right or wrong in a situation where society has led human to depoliticize. He only acts and finds no reason for his actions. With a logic that considers truth dead and completely relativistic, that person will be more likely to justify his actions and will not seek the truth at all, or anything close to the truth. Human will not understand himself until he seeks to discover the closest thing to the truth, and human who does not know his individual identity will have no understanding of collective identity and Otherness. There is a close relationship between identity and truth. Without identity, there is no truth, and where there is no truth, anonymity shows itself.

The way forward for human is to think about the self. By looking at history, by taking refuge in art, by understanding philosophy, by perusing mythology and cultures, human can see his true face in the mirror and visualize another in the mirror.

The aim of Hermes Magazine is to present beauty and glory to its audience in the form of words, and by publishing the different ideas of writers from different countries and cultures, to some extent represent the true nature of human societies. We are very happy that you are the reader of this magazine and you are following us.

YOUR FRIEND,

Mohammad Abedi

Contents

Philosophy

Mythology

Literature

Art History

Other Articles

Poetry

Short Story

PHILOSOPHY

TWO KINDS OF LABOR — AND OF PEOPLE

BY THOMAS POGGE

Human beings meet their needs through labor — their own and that of others. The labor of mothers, peasants, builders, factory and transport workers, doctors and nurses, educators and researchers, artists and entertainers, engineers and planners. Such productive labor provides goods and services that, directly or indirectly, fulfill human needs.

Then there is predatory labor, labor that does not provide goods or services for the fulfillment of human needs but rather appropriates the fruits of others' productive labor. This includes much of the labor of burglars and warriors, slave holders and arms dealers, priests and nobles, speculators, investors and wealth managers, lawyers and accountants, politicians and lobbyists. To be sure, such labor can be quite valuable, as when one group of warriors or lawyers fiercely protects your body or rights from another such group. Still, this is hardly a reason for wanting such predatory labor around at all.

As humankind becomes ever more productive, an ever-larger share of the fruits of productive labor can sustainably be appropriated by predatory labor. Insofar as this can happen, it usually does happen, because experts in predation tend to do better in the competition over the social product than its producers. This is so for two systematic reasons. First, they are much better trained and prepared for such competition because redistribution is the center of their professional expertise. For tax lawyers, speculators or lobbyists, it is the essence of their job to bend the distribution of wealth or political influence in favor of themselves or their paying clients. Peasants, builders, teachers, physicians and engineers, by contrast, are not trained for, or professionally occupied with, such redistribution but rather with producing food, care, learning, buildings, tools and machines. This first reason makes it likely that predatory labor wins superior rewards within most social systems.

Such superior rewards, in turn, bring the second reason into play: winning superior rewards, predatory labor then also attracts a disproportional share of the most creative and energetic people. The brightest young minds then dream of being a priest rather than peasant, banker rather than engineer, lawyer rather than doctor, investor rather than inventor, politician rather than artist. To be sure, some bright young minds will still want to be teachers, artists or scientists even if they could earn much more on Wall Street or K Street. [1]. But most will "sell out" and thereby contribute their superior talents to further increase the capacity of predatory labor to capture large and increasing shares of the social product.

----

[1] Wall Street is the symbolic center of the financial district of New York City. K Street in Washington D.C. houses many lobbying firms that seek to influence politicians and so-called civil servants.

This tendency for the best and the brightest to drift toward predatory labor is supported by several familiar phenomena of moral psychology. There is the common thought that one's own predatory labor "makes no difference" because any harm it does would otherwise be done by someone else. Then there is the popular sucker exemption according to which one cannot be morally required to disadvantage oneself vis-à-vis others through moral self-restraint ("others are doing it, so why can't I?"). Once one has taken on a predatory labor role, one's commitment is further reinforced by peer pressures in one's social environment and by the self-blinkering thought that one "is merely doing one's job." Additional reinforcement comes from the fact that those who engage in predatory labor tend to use their strong social position to promote a societal ethos that makes income and wealth, regardless of their source, the foremost basis of social recognition. Because their predatory labor can hardly be presented as admirable, they favor a culture where respect and attributions of success are based on income, wealth and spending. Such a culture is then further entrenched through a human psychological tendency that has been extensively researched under the heading the belief in a just world: our judgments of the moral character and conduct of people are significantly affected by clearly morally irrelevant information about their wellbeing: when people are doing well, we are inclined to think that they are good people; when they are doing poorly, we tend to think that they must be deserving it on account of some flaws in their conduct or character. [2].

We have seen how, as societies become richer, they come to be increasingly dominated by those who do predatory labor and increasingly permeated by a culture that assigns social worth on the basis of money. How dangerous and destructive these two trends are, becomes apparent when we reflect on how deeply the values, understandings and emotions of persons are shaped by their professional roles and interests, and on how dramatically the interests associated with many predatory–labor roles diverge from any plausible conception of the common good. Eager to increase their profits and influence, military contractors and arms dealers are longing for tensions and arms races, for hostilities and wars as conditions in which their business can thrive — and they make efforts to promote such conditions. To be sure, they do not want an all–out nuclear war that would destroy life on this planet. But they do work toward a world on the brink of war, a world of high distrust in which trillions are spent on war games and weapons of mass destruction. Such a world comes with a lot of low–level violence and continuous small risks of serious devastation. But, military contractors and arms dealers perceive these costs and risks as acceptable and present them as necessary for national security. [3].

----

[2] The locus classicus is Melvin J. Lerner, The Belief in a Just World. A Fundamental Delusion. New York: Plenum Press 1980.

[3] Some introductory information about arms industry lobbying in the United States and Europe can be found, respectively, at https://www.huffpost.com/entry/arms-industry-ramps-up-lo_b_7484338 and https://corporateeurope.org/en/power-lobbies/2017/12/arms-industry-lobbying-and-militarisation-eu.

The professional interest of politicians also gravitates toward hostility and tension. When ordinary citizens perceive their country to be threatened by nasty rivals, they feel insecure and tend to follow and support their political leaders. This tendency to "rally around the flag" especially benefits the executive branch of government which gains status against the other branches whenever there is a heightened danger of violence. Even if the top officials of the executive and the armed forces would not benefit from a bloody shooting war, they nonetheless understand that their own political power is enhanced by vivid awareness that such a war is a real possibility. Damaged political leaders are often sorely tempted to lead their country to the brink of war to save or enhance their position, something that can be done openly or also by stealth or misinformation (creating the false appearance that our country has been wronged or threatened or attacked by others). And the aggressive postures associated with being on the brink of war then make actual war and violence substantially more likely. [4].

Speculators make money on big swings in markets, so they have a professional interest in instability. This interest is initially passive: speculators try to sniff out especially volatile markets and then build positions in such markets in the direction in which they expect the next big move to occur. Once such a position has been built, the interest becomes more active as speculators are then inclined to look for ways to make their chosen market more volatile and to trigger a major market move in their own favor. This can be done through rumors, for example, or through clandestine or tacit collaborations designed to move markets. Through such machinations, full-time professional speculators and traders can most easily fleece amateur market participants, such as farmers who sell futures contracts to reduce their market risk or retail investors who own stocks to pay for their future retirement. Big market moves involve massive redistributions from the amateurs to the professionals, as amply documented in records of trading desk profits. Some such market swings seem to have no comprehensible external reasons — just some professionals finding it in their interest to rock the boat, often in team work. In other cases, such external reasons do exist — the COVID-19 pandemic for instance — but even there the professionals are seeking to exacerbate profitable volatility, thereby destabilizing markets and often causing severe losses to less-savvy market participants. Such unsophisticated participants can include whole states, as exemplified in the currency markets whose volume is a staggering 19 times that of the gross world product. [5]. Among the countries whose currencies have been devastated by

----

[4] The seminal essay on this subject is John Mueller, "Presidential Popularity from Truman to Johnson," American Political Science Review 64:1 (1970), pp. 18–34. For a later, expanded and more empirical treatment, see Dieuwertje Kuijpers, "Rally around All the Flags: The Effect of Military Casualties on Incumbent Popularity in Ten Countries 1990–2014," Foreign Policy Analysis 15:3 (2019), pp. 392–412.

[5] Assuming 253 trading days annually, the currency markets have annual turnover of about USD 1,800 trillion. The value of all goods and services produced worldwide presently sums to about USD 94 trillion per year.

speculative attacks in recent decades, causing vast disruptions and impoverishment to their populations, are India (1991), Mexico (1994), Thailand (1997, with Indonesia, South Korea, Laos, Malaysia and the Philippines also dragged in), Russia (1998 and 2014), Ecuador (1998–9), Argentina (1999–2002), Brazil (1999), Turkey (2001 and 2018), and Uruguay (2002). [6].

As a final example, tax lawyers and accountants have a professional interest that the tax environment be highly complex and ever–changing. Pursuing this shared interest, they have been promoting a world with a huge diversity of complex and frequently–revised national tax regimes which afford rich individuals and corporations endless opportunities for tax evasion and abuse. To exploit these opportunities, a huge global industry has sprung up of tax havens, secrecy jurisdictions, letterbox companies, fake trusts and anonymous accounts, along with an army of shady lawyers, accountants, lobbyists, financial advisors and other facilitators. This netherworld of global finance is estimated to manage over USD 30 trillion in wealth, equivalent to about 7% of all private financial wealth or one–third of the annual gross world product. [7]. As recently revealed — by LuxLeaks (2014), Panama Papers (2015), Bahamas Leaks (2016), Paradise Papers (2017), Cayman Leak (2019) etc. — this sophisticated infrastructure facilitates not merely massive tax abuse, but also crimes of many other kinds such as illegal trade in persons, drugs and weapons, embezzlement, international terrorism, hacking of democracy, and the money laundering associated with all such activities. In these ways, the global haven industry massively aggravates

----

[6] For general introduction, see https://www.encyclopedia.com/social-sciences-and-law/economics-business-and-labor/money-banking-and-investment/speculation. A more detailed analysis is provided by Marco Di Maggio, "Market Turmoil and Destabilizing Speculation," Columbia Business School Research Paper No. 13–80 (August 1, 2016), available at https://ssrn.com/abstract=2353133. On the important special case of food markets, see Olivier de Schutter, "Food Commodities Speculation and Food Price Crises: Regulation to Reduce the Risk of Price Volatility," Briefing Note 02. United Nations Special Rapporteur on the Right to Food, 2010, pp. 1–14, at www.srfood.org/images/stories/pdf/otherdocuments/20102309_briefing_note_02_en_ok.pdf; and also MarcoLagi, Yavni Bar–Yam, Karla Bertrand and Yaneer Bar–Yam, 'The Food Crises: A Quantitative Model of Food Prices Including Speculators and Ethanol Conversion" (September 22, 2011), available at https://papers.ssrn.com/sol3/papers.cfm?abstract_id=1932247.

[7] See https://financialtransparency.org/wp-content/uploads/2016/12/FTC_infographic_20170202_Eng.pdf for a brief introduction. A credible estimate of USD 24–36 trillion is provided by James Henry, "Let's Tax Anonymous Wealth! A Modest Proposal to Reduce Inequality, Attack Organized Crime, Aid Developing Countries, and Raise Badly Needed Revenue from the World's Wealthiest Tax Dodgers, Kleptocrats, and Felons," in Thomas Pogge and Krishen Mehta, eds., Global Tax Fairness, Oxford, Oxford University Press 2016, pp. 48 and 79. For reasons Henry gives (p. 79), the estimate by Zucman seems too low/restrictive. See Gabriel Zucman, The Hidden Wealth of Nations, Chicago, University of Chicago Press 2015. Aggregate global household wealth is estimated at USD 418.3 trillion at the end of 2020. See Anthony Shorrocks, Jim Davies and Rodrigo Lluberas, Global Wealth Report 2021, Credit Suisse Research Institute, Zürich 2020, pp. 5 and 7, also available at https://www.credit-suisse.com/about-us/en/reports-research/global-wealth-report.html.

national and global inequalities and greatly impedes the development of poorer countries by enabling multinational corporations, autocrats, corrupt politicians and officials, millionaires and criminals to drain them of capital and tax revenues. The Washington NGO Global Financial Integrity estimates that such illicit financial outflows from developing countries amount to USD 1.1 trillion each year. [8]. The global haven industry also serves to store an immense amount of hidden wealth that can be deployed for corrupt purposes, in particular for corrupting the procedures and officers of states and corporations.

Summing up, this brief paper supports two main conclusions:

1.While the role-specific interests of productive labor tend to be reasonably well-aligned with the long-term collective interest of humankind in stable peace, prosperity and ecological balance, the role-specific interests of predatory labor often dramatically diverge from that common interest and are also much more short-term.

2.The governance institutions that determine social organization and infrastructure on all levels — global, regional, national and subnational — are heavily dominated by people in predatory-labor roles, who constitute a minority of human beings but a large and increasing preponderance of political power.

These two points help explain and predict increasing economic, social and political inequality with associated persistence of severe poverty, as well as increasing instability with the associated grave dangers of highly destructive wars and ecological disaster.

Our fate is not sealed. But, to change it, great concerted efforts are required on the part of the majority in productive labor. As a first step, we must put away the belief that those who govern us are "sitting in the same boat" and are pursuing a vision of humanity's future that is broadly aligned with our values and ideals. For the most part, these people have no vision for humanity's future at all, but a myopic obsession with amassing wealth and power in competition with one another. This becomes apparent when one looks beneath the thin veneer of staged professionalism to behold the stunning incompetence of those in power, illustrated by the response to COVID-19, for instance, or by the 20-year U.S. occupation of Afghanistan, which wasted an inconceivable USD 2.26 trillion. [9]. The next steps then involve the fight for democratizing politics and against entrenched systemic injustices — tasks I have begun to reflect upon elsewhere.

----

[8] Global Financial Integrity: Trade-Related Illicit Financial Flows in 135 Developing Countries: 2008–2017, GFI, Washington D.C., March 2020. Available at https://gfintegrity.org/report/trade-related-illicit-financial-flows-in-135-developing-countries-2008-2017/.

[9] See detailed study by Brown University's Watson Institute of International and Public Affairs at watson.brown.edu/costsofwar/figures/2021/human-and-budgetary-costs-date-us-war-afghanistan-2001-2021. This amount is USD 18,400 per U.S. household and could have paid for half the worldwide cost of achieving the Sustainable Development Goals, intended to eradicate severe poverty by 2030. See Jeffrey Sachs et al., SDG Costing and Financing for Low-Income Developing Countries, New York, Sustainable Development Solutions Network 2019, at https://sdgfinancing.unsdsn.org/static/files/sdg-costing-and-finance-for-LIDCS.pdf.

ARCESILAUS AGAINTS THE EPISTEMOLOGY OF STOICS

BY AYBÜKE FAYETÖRBAY

Abstract

Debates on the criterion of truth have been one of the basic debates of epistemology since Ancient Greece. The aim of this study is to discuss Arkesilaos' answer against the Phantasia cataleptic argument of Stoics and the source of knowledge and the criterion of truth in terms of the concept to eulogon.

Keywords: Epistemology, Stoics, Arcesilaos, phantasia, phantasia kataleptike, to eulogon.

Is there a need for knowledge for a good life and a truth criterion for knowledge? If so, can we define a truth criterion and explain how it works?

 Discussions about the source of information have been going on for a long time. There has been this debate since Ancient Greece, when the philosophy of knowledge first emerged. Although the Ancient Greek term ἐπιστήμη (epistémē) means knowledge in its general use, it is more accurate to say that this concept is a knowledge system that defines the objects on a specific era and in a restricted area since the criterion of what is true and what is knowledge differs in each school.

The first school to be dealt with in the context of this study on the source of information and the criterion of truth is Stoicism. "At the beginning of 200 BC, we are in Athens. As a bearded Phoenician walks around the agora, a crowd rushes around to listen to him. This person being the Zenith of Kition, became the center of the movement after leaving Plato's Academy, which would become the most important philosophical school of the Hellenistic era."[1]. Stoic philosophy is one of the most prominent schools of philosophy of the Hellenistic period. Knowledge is possible for stoeticians. There is a truth criterion. Stoicists argue that the source of knowledge is experimentatiton. The source of human knowledge and reason is experiment, more specifically sensation or sensory perception. The effect of objects on the human soul is roughly a material-physical effect. What makes this possible is the existence of a group of impressions that are inherently correct and cannot be incorrect, and therefore can form the basis of knowledge. Here we come across the concept of phantasia. The concept of Phantasia should be distinguished from phantastikon. Phantastikon is a movement without an object. Phantasia has a designed object.

----

[1] Umberto Eco, çev. Leyla Tonguç Basmacı, Antik Yunan, Alfa, İstanbul 2018, s.526.

For stoaisians, phantasia is the first stage of the transformation of experience into knowledge. Phantasia is the representation in the subject of the encounter of the object. The object encountered with sensation is reflected in the mind of the subject as a design. "Zenon defined perception as an impression (phantasia) in the soul, and Kleanthes took that definition as it was, and compared the impression that occurred in the soul to the stampthat a seal left on the wax. According to him, just as a seal stamps on wax, the objects of the outer world also stamp on the sensory organs, leaving their mark"[2]. According to Zenon, nature has been established in a way to let human reach knowledge. The starting point and source of the information is phantasia. The concept of phantasia, which Stoics regard as the starting point and source of knowledge, is impressions, but not every impression has the same value in terms of knowledge and truth. Zenon says that there is a third mental state between doxa[3] and knowledge called catalepsis[4]. Catalepsis is the mental state between doxa and knowledge. The difference between catalepsis and doxa is that catalepsis is absolutely true as opposed to doxa. Catalepsis is the first step of knowledge and is a criterion of truth. If understanding is not shaken, it is knowledge. "We must remember that what is right for the Stoics is the mirror of what is true and what exists since they are the starting point of representations. On the other hand, intelligence gives the subject the ability to distinguish representations from each other and to choose which one to give approval to (synkatathesis). Only representations that Stoics define as concepts (kataleptikai) deserve approval."[5].

Zenon calls these impressions that clearly and distinctly grasp the absolutely reliable object in terms of information, phantasia cataleptic. Phantasia cataleptic is the confirmation of the impression. The mind must first make an impression through sensory perceptions, whether or not to give this consent in the process of generating information. For stoists, impression is not a simple physical affection of sensory organs, but a concept that becomes a meaningful perception that is approved by the mind. According to stoicists, approval is given to the content of the impression. Therefore, for the purpose of obtaining knowledge, objects first come to the sensory organs and produce impressions. The mind then becomes effective and this impression is given an approval or a rejection. The understanding of the approved impression is catalepsy. Catalepsis is a condition that the impression has not yet discovered. The final stage is the transformation of catalepsy into information. This is phantasia cataleptic.

----

[2] Ahmet Arslan, İlkçağ Felsefe Tarihi 4, İstanbul Bilgi Üniversitesi Yayınları, İstanbul 2012, s.242.

[3] doxa: is the association of hegemonicon (reasoning), which is perceived through sensory organs and therefore subject to the determinations of the body (soma), the domain of the thought.

[4] κατάληψις (katalepsis): comprehension, comprehension. For Stoicists; Doxa- Catalepsis- Information.

[5] Umberto Eco, çev. Leyla Tonguç Basmacı, Antik Yunan, Alfa, İstanbul 2018, s.530.

Zenon explains this dialectic in an analogy. [6].

According to Zenon, an impression resembles an open hand. Zenon show the second stage by closing his palm a little. This stage shows the response to the impression. In the third stage, he closes his hand completely and makes a fist. This is the understanding of the impression. In the final stage, Zenon grasps his hand, which has become a fist, with the other. This is now truly grasping the impression.

Impression (Phantasia) – Approval(Synkatathesis) - Thrust -> Action

According to stoicists, approval is given to the content of the impression. Thrust follows approval. For approval to occur, that object must be viewed as something specific. For example, only the impression of the fruit is not sufficient for an action to occur, that fruit should be seen as something. That fruit should be seen as something that will satisfy hunger.

 If comprehension is the perception of the truth as it is, it must be the impressions that bring it to us as it is. What if one can't grasp anything? What happens if a right impression is the same as a false impression? Can it be shown that there are right impressions that are unlike any other false impression that is not the same as itself? Are there true impressions that are too similar to the false impressions to distinguish them?

Zenon thinks that the right impressions, the processes of the emergence of these cataleptic impressions, mark them in a very specific, distinctive way. However, Arkesilaos, an influential critic of Stoic epistemology, has objections to this. He argues that there is nothing that prevents the impression from something that is right and the impression from something that is not correct to be exactly the same. Like Socrates and Piron, Arkesilaos wrote nothing. We receive information about him mainly from the skeptical philosophers Cicero and Sextus Empiricus. The main source of his way of life is Diogenes Laertius. "Arkesilaos is the founder of the Middle Akademia. He was the first philosopher to avoid judgment because of contradictory evidence."[7].

For stoicists, the mind is the sum of repeated impressions. Concepts arise from repeated impressions. Therefore, the starting point of knowledge is sensory impressions. For Zenon, the criterion of truth is phantasia cataleptic. This is the main objection of Arkesilaos. He offers two arguments against Zenon's argument for grasping impressions as a measure of truth:

1. Objects that are indistinguishably similar.

2. Unhealthy mental states.

----

[6] Academia, 2, 145.

[7] Diogenes Laertios, çev. Candan Şentuna, Ünlü Filozofların Yaşamları ve Öğretileri, Yapı Kredi Yayınları, İstanbul 2013, s.188.

According to Arkesilaos, there is no right impression so that there is no false impression that cannot be confused with it." [8]. For example, think about twins. Twins that are indistinguishable from each other can cause a false impression. Zenon argues that a real pomegranate and the wax figure of a pomegranate leaves the same mark on our soul. If what Zenon said was true, then the twins should not be confused, and in the pomegranate example the impression of a real pomegranate and the wax pomegranate should be distinguished. The second part is about dreams, illusions, or abnormal states of mind, such as Heracles. [9]. In both cases it is always possible to have the same false impression as the real impression at the same time. Therefore, it does not seem possible to say that the impression of the right thing is different or distinguishable from the impression of the wrong one. Therefore, no impression can be guaranteed by itself because of the way its content is represented. We can confirm a truly correct impression, as well as validate impressions that are not.

According to Arkesilaos, we encounter things and an impression occurs. This impression stimulates an impulse. This impulse naturally leads us to what we need spontaneously. Therefore, the ranking in Arkesilaos is:

Impression(Phantasia) - Thrust -> Action

So it is irrationalized by removing the approval(syncatathesis).

Arcesilaos says that as a practical criterion, instead of approval, one can act on a reasonable basis, ie to eulogon. Arkesilaos describes the practical criterion to distinguish successful action as being reasonable (to eulogon). "In this way, Arkesilaos argued that the person who suspended his judgment on everything could still make choices or abstain on the basis of being reasonable, and could take actions." [10]. To take the right action, simply follow what is reasonable. This will be a virtuous act and will lead to happiness. Reasonability is a concept of Stoics. Arkesilaos' method is not a theoretical claim, but a dialectic that simply points to a phenomenon with examples. Why should Arkesilaos use the notion of Stoicism as a plausible argument and save the Stoics? At this point, two concepts emerge:

1. Katorthoma

2. Kathekon

----

[8] Ahmet Arslan, İlkçağ Felsefe Tarihi 4, İstanbul Bilgi Üniversitesi Yayınları, İstanbul 2012, s.469.

[9] In the story, also known as Hercules, Heracles killed his own children as a result of his mind not being able to distinguish false impressions. If the right impression were distinguishable from the false impression, Heracles should not have confirmed the false impression which his mind fully approved, saw clearly and distinctly, which ultimately led to the killing of his own children.

[10] Ahmet Arslan, İlkçağ Felsefe Tarihi 4, İstanbul Bilgi Üniversitesi Yayınları, İstanbul 2012, s.474.

Katorthoma, is the perfect action of knowledge, the right action. The concept of Kathekon is the non-wise. Arkesilaos defines correct action as actions that can be rationally explained after rationalization. This definition is actually the definition of kathekon in Stoics. Here the concept that Arkesilaos uses to describe the right action is in fact the perfect action of the Stoics, in other words the kind of action that the sage would actually do. The wise possible action for the Stoicists seems to be not so wise. Therefore, the actions of the cataleptic type between good and evil can be such actions that are not so wise.

As a result; According to the stoicists, approval is given to the content of the impression and the impulse follows a rational act. For all kinds of actions, it is necessary to approve the impressions related to that action. According to stoicists, only kataleptike deserves approval. For stoeticians, phantasia is the confirmation of kataleptike impression. The criterion of truth is phantasia cataleptic. The ranking of the Stoicists on the road to action:

Impression (Phantasia) - Approval (Synkatathesis) - Impulse -> Action.

Arkesilaos' objection is about the approval part of this ranking. No impression can be guaranteed by itself because of the way its content is represented. Therefore, in addition to a correct impression, a false impression can also be confirmed as true. For this reason, the ranking in Arkesilaos:

Impression - Thrust -> Action

is irrationalized by subtracting confirmation.So what Arkesilaos suggests is this: A wise act would be good, as the Stoics say, but we have to settle for the second best. For the Stoics this is a problem, but for Arkesilos there is no problem, because there is no need for approval for action. Instead of approval, to eulogon is the practical criterion. The reasonable is justified by the practical criterion without approval, because Arcesilaus assumes that action is possible based on reasonable opinions that do not lead to faith. In the context of action, the wise person can be considered to accept the reasonable (to eulogon) without having a cognitive impression of how things are.

Bibliography

ARSLAN, A. İlkçağ Felsefe Tarihi 4, İstanbul Bilgi Üniversitesi Yayınları, İstanbul.
ECO,U. (2018). Antik Yunan, çev. Leyla Tonguç Basmacı, Alfa Yayınları, İstanbul.

LAERTIOS, D. (2013). Ünlü Filozofların Yaşamları ve Öğretileri, çev. Candan Şentuna, Yapı Kredi Yayınları, İstanbul.

LIDDELL H.G. and SCOTT, R. Greek- English Lexicon, Clarendon Press-Oxford.

https://plato.stanford.edu

MYTHOLOGY

THAT WHICH IS NOT: SHIVA

BY SHRISHTI PATEL

A god of Nothingness?

As modern science today has approved the theory that everything comes from nothing and eventually goes to nothing and the basis of existence and fundamental quality of cosmos is vast nothingness. The galaxies, planets etc. are small sprinkling of existential colours on the grand canvass of infinitely empty space which is referred to as Shiva. Shiva literally means "that which is not" or "nothingness" which is the womb from which everything is born and also the oblivion into which everything will be sucked back. In Hinduism there are many names and attributes to this supreme divine like Shankar ("beneficent"), Mahesh or Mahadev ("great god"), Natrajan ("a cosmic dancer"), Adiyogi ("the first yogi"), Sanharak ("the destroyer") etc. Shiva is formless, which means Shiva can assume all forms at will and is the pivot on which the entire universe turns. Shiva connects the forms to no

form; he is the fulcrum, the tangent between infinity and zero. He is described as a non being (not as a being); still quite contradicting fact is that we have a face for even nothingness which might have originated from the tendency of human mind to picture everything. We tend not to believe most of the things which are not exposed to our eyes so we colour the images to form a meaningful interpretation of our thoughts and maybe this is why our ancestors came up with giving a face to' that which is not' and as far as the Hindu mythology goes Shiva is usually depicted in painting and sculptures as a man with calm face and blue neck(as he is said to hold the poison in his throat that emerged from the churning of the cosmic ocean) and ashes of corpses that are smeared on his body, his hair arranged in a coil of matted locks (jatamukuta) along with moon and Ganges (the sacred river of India) placed on his head, wearing garland of skulls and serpents around his neck, has a trident("trishul") in one hand describing him also as a great warrior and a hand drum("damru") in the other one justifying his state as the 'lord of the dance'. Shiva has three eyes, the third eye which is capable of burning destruction when focused outward. Being India's most auspicious aspect of divinity there are various stories describing his wisdom, bravery and divinity which is usual but today let's look at something more than just the stories, where we look beyond the surfaces of these appearances, shapes, and temples.

Let's look on the part when he is also referred to as "Adiyogi" or the first yogi or guru who is the basis of what we now know as yogic science today. Yoga is not only about headstand and fitness regime rather it originated as science to know the essential nature of life, how it is created and how it can be taken to its ultimate possibility. In the yogic culture, Shiva is not known as a God but as the "Adiyogi" or the first Yogi. It is said that around 15,000 years ago he started performing an intense dance in the Himalayas, where the Lord resides. Lord Shiva's intense dance would range from dancing wildly to sitting still. Looking at his performance, the "Sapta Rishis" or the seven sages who watched him perform were astounded. The first part of Shiva's teaching was to his wife Parvati. He refers to her as the most gracious and beautiful performer. Shiva then transformed himself into the Adi Guru on the day that is now celebrated as Guru Purnima and began the next session of the yogic teaching with the "Sapta Rishis" on the banks of 'Kanti Sarovar', near Kedarnath. An influx of pilgrims attend these holy shrines regularly even today where the yogis still perform the art of yoga.

Shiva is both "that which is not" which is not a being and "adiyogi" which is a man. This seems weird at first to hear but logically thinking it's possible because when you call someone yogi that means he has experienced the existence himself and if you have to contain the existence within you even for a moment as an experience, you have to be that nothingness. Only nothingness can hold everything. Something can never hold everything. A vessel can't hold an ocean, a planet can hold ocean but can't contain the sun .While a solar system can hold the sun but not the whole the rest of galaxy. So progressively thinking this way, eventually we see that there is to experience everything you first need to be nothing. 'Yoga' means 'union' which means that a yogi who has experienced the union, even for a moment has been absolute nothingness. So in a way they are synonyms yet two very different aspects.

While Shiva is the originator of this entire universe, his wife Shakti is the primordial cosmic energy that represents the dynamic forces that are thought to move through the entire universe. Shakti or energy manifests itself as consciousness. Consciousness, the manifested gives us the ability to perceive and experience. Shiva has no form, but Shiva takes form of everything that we perceive and that which all perceive. Shakti or energy is what brings the mind out of the body. This divine couple are called to be inseparable because there union is the very basis of the existence of everything. Shakti is also worshiped in Hinduism through many names as Parvati, sati, kali etc.

Shiva is the absolute, connected to "energy or Shakti" that manifests for all possibility and that which projects relativity. Therefore it is the divine but not in its religious sense but in a sense that it has no existence. Shiva Shakti creates patterns within chaos; creates complexity from simplicity beyond the perception of dimensions. Depend not on the kingdom of God, for the kingdom of God resides in you; Shiva resides in you. Symbolism is a derivative of the scriptures; but a symbol has no meaning unless it is a part of you. What we seek is what exists and that what does not exist, is all that exists; that which nothing is. Nothingness is not an excuse to run away from reality, but should be an excuse to experience reality. Physical reality is mathematically difficult to understandbecause of thechaos within it,but the non-physicalreality is simple,non-mathematical and a construct of nothing from which we emerge.

All phenomena around us that we observe and perceive depend on the level and the extent of perception we are given access to. If perception has to evolve, energy has to evolve. The nothingness within has to transform to everything to seek the Shiva and enjoy the Shakti in oneself. The physical has to be understood as a emergence from the non-physical; thatwhich exists beyondthe limits ofperception and manifestation. Shiva Shakti is neither good nor bad; nothingness is neither good nor bad, our perceptions create good and bad,our greed createsgood and bad,our selfishness createsgood and bad.Shiva as nothingness holdsthe energy orShakti that createsand destroys wherefrom this chaoswe emerge from thisone source. Wetherefore need touse our imaginationsto explore the un manifested; the true reality of our very own existence that resides in each one of us. I know it is easy to look at a picture or sculpture and believe in god and worship but it takes a lot of divinity and devotion to look into a vast space of nothingness and believe in that formless energy. We need to think within the void to understand what emerges from the void. That is the reason we are gifted with consciousness, a manifestation from the void, where we get an opportunity to look into the void; the Shiva in us.

LITERATURE

VICTOR HUGO AND EMILE ZOLA: LITERARY HISTORIANS

BY MADILYN GRACE PHELPS

The relationship between literature and history can best be described as the classically familiar fun sibling/responsible sibling. Guess which is which? Except, one would not associate the names Victor Hugo and Emile Zola with "fun." They are some of the premier writers of the 19th century, writing strong works with social and political themes. But they are remembered as the strong novelists they were, their fictional worlds so vivid and heart-wrenching that one could not help but see themselves in the likes of Quasimodo, Etienne, Catherine, Fantine and even Claude Frollo or Inspector Javert. This was no accident on the authors' part.

The Trojan Horse was a literal device used in ancient wartime military strategy, but the meaning has evolved into a metaphor for conveying a message hidden in something grand. This is perfectly applicable to Hugo and Zola. These two were unabashed in their principles and political motivations, both in their private lives and in their writings. This comes out through their attention to detail; focus on human behavior and an ingrained social inequity they live with.

In their works, Notre Dame de Paris and Germinal, respectively, they hit back against Napoleonic and clerical rule and the exploitation of poor, working class people. Often this went hand in hand, as the state system for education dictated disciplined and militaristic approaches, Latin and no geography or history of France's place in the world. Patrizia Lombardo dissected Napoleon's Regime being drilled down to "disciple, obedience, hierarchy… direct and determine how the new generations thought: the state would never build up a nation with a stable political identity if the young people were not told to be republican or monarchist, irreligious or Catholic. If the state did not monopolize public education, it would constantly confront disorder and change." The strict, ritualistic ethos of Catholicism influenced the organization of society and especially the education system, reinstating clerical order and bureaucracy, the very thing that led to the bloody Reign of Terror. Zola extensively interviewed and got to know the mining families in a small village and bore witness to their pain and resigned acceptance but possessing a human dignity and familial duty on their backs. Such a description of their personal, admirable qualities in such a context is the unique space this occupies, that branch between romanticism and political treatise. Even in their darkest hour, the miners as a whole did not turn on each other and held fast during disaster while their families were enduring supporters, during their strike and the climactic mining collapse.

These men are exceptionally intelligent. We know that. They knew the normal reader could digest their novels/political manifestos covertly and keep out of sight of the church authorities.

This freedom in their prose comes from their melding of grotesque and picturesque imagery, including spiritual essence, personified setting spaces (Notre Dame, the mines) and beautiful writing about horrible situations. These traits added to the theses made on the connection between justice and social class. Essentially, those lower on the social strata receive little mercy from the justice system. Conversely, the wealthy frequently received far better fortunes than what was deserving, although not everyone is as evil or uncaring as Claude Frollo or the bourgeois mine-owner in Zola's Germinal. Although Victor Hugo defined Claude Frollo as the epitome of evil: hypocritical, powerful, ascetic, bullying, abusing his own power to hurt others. He lusts after a young woman, abuses his charge and casts a ruthless judgement on those deemed beneath him. The malice in Hugo's characterization comes from that Claude Frollo sounds like a human man. These authors were screaming to the people through their oeuvres, "The real villain or true evil is not the devil or an abstract monster. The real monsters are human beings."

To be clear, what is found literature and fiction is not primary evidence to draw reasonable conclusions about any sort of historical event. How these events or patterns covered in fiction and how they are characterized by the authors can speak to the social or political weight of the period and the political stances of the author. 19th century France was rife with a barely stable bureaucracy, a neglected underclass and clerical precedence over reason, even after the Enlightenment. These men and their works depict the conditions of the day to point out the injustice and makes heroes out of ordinary people. People we may recognize or see on the street every day. Not morally perfect, but not deserving of the harsh hand their birthplace, class or ethnicity wrought them. These are pleas for a radical revolution based on tenets of humanism and an acknowledgement of the potential for darkness in every human being, in order to get back into the light.

Bibliography:

Hugo, Victor. Notre Dame de Paris (1832). Trans. Alban Krailsheimer. Oxford: Oxford University Press. 2009.

Lombardo, Patrizia. "Discipline and Melancholy." A New History of French Literature. Cambridge, Mass.: Harvard University Press, 1994.

Zola, Emile. Germinal (1885). Trans. Roger Pearson. London: Penguin Classic Publishing. 2004.

GIVING CHOCOLATE MABBIE A CHANCE

BY STEPHANIE MARRIE

It seems today that, according to critic Randall Jarrell, modern readers do not understand older poems, particularly those of the old Western canon, because of "their systematic unreceptiveness" of the poem's language and subject (9). After all, in order to better understand a poem's meaning and its effect on readers, they need "willing emotional empathy" (Jarrell 9). However, I want to bring up racial unreceptiveness, or the white American misconception of racial progress. It is a fairly common idea among young Americans that racism ended with the civil rights movement. Thus, when African Americans bring up current instances of racism, they are hesitant to believe that it still pervades society at large. I hope to dispel this misconception by discussing the poem "the ballad of chocolate Mabbie" by Gwendolyn Brooks; this poem captures one of the most insidious prejudices against African Americans, so subtle that even other African Americans perpetuate them. In this poem, a young black girl named Mabbie is in love with Willie Boon, but he is with a lighter-skinned African American (or lynx, as was the old slang for black person). Though Jarrell claims, "When you begin to read a poem you are entering a foreign country whose laws and language and life are a kind of translation of your own," (9) I would argue that this poem is meaningful not because it translates its experience to the non-black reader's life, but it forces the reader to realize its black girl perspective.

The poem's obscurity lies not in its language, but in its subject matter: racist rejection. As a popular form, the ballad's language is simple and thus easy for the everyday reader to understand. It also handles its rhyme casually every second line, matching "seven" with "heaven," etc. But notice how the rhyming lines tells the reader where Mabbie stands in regard to the racial dynamic of choosing a mate. The lines "And Mabbie was all of seven" and "And Mabbie thought life was heaven" reveal how young and innocent she and her outlook are, making her later rejection seem all the more cruel to the reader (lines 2, 4). It sets up the world that will soon be shattered by the racial reality of beauty standards. But notice the word "heaven," a place that is usually thought of as nothing but white clouds. Then the line right after has the grammar school's "pearly gates;" pearly gates are also associated with heaven. Pearly is a word synonymous with white and shiny. The word choice demonstrates how white-centered Mabbie's world is; yet she does not know how this white-centeredness will affect her. Then the next two rhyming lines, "And it cannot be too long" and "That carry the bubble of song!" pairs inevitability with innocence (lines 14, 16). Again, these lines demonstrate that the idea that a black girl will have to wake up to the bleak reality sooner or later is all the more tragic because of how naïve she is. The reader is once more invited to pity Mabbie and then wake up to the racially coded dating world. The final rhyming lines "Yet chocolate companions had she:" and "Mabbie on Mabbie to be" really hammers the message that this is not an isolated incident, but a widespread problem facing darker skinned girls, and thus the reader's eyes may be opened to this bigger problem and see how unjust it is (lines 22, 24).

Ballads are known for repetition of names and epithets. In fact, the repetition of the name Mabbie throughout the poem hammers home the fact that Mabbie is not just one person, but she represents all those other dark girls who were passed up for light-skinned girls. Thus, the ballad form helps to bring the message into the reader's potentially unreceptive head. The last phrase "to be" also suggests that this unfavorable comparison may happen again in the future (line 24). The subject matter, being unrequited love, may be easy to relate to, but the way in which it is implemented in poem reveals a very specific perspective. The poem transcends its potential obscurity and manages to get across this perspective, foreign to a non-black reader, through its simple language and repetition.

I anticipate the reader's potential alienation with this poem's subject matter because of my personal inability to fully understand Mabbie's heartbreak. I am a light-skinned girl, being born from a Japanese mother and a white father. My mother has often complimented my fair skin, particularly my clear forehead. I have been called pale before, but never in a negative sense. Mabbie, on the other hand, clearly has dark skin, being "cut from a chocolate bar," (line 3) and is implicitly rejected for it. We never see her crush tell her off, but he happily exits the grammar school one afternoon with "a lemon-hued lynx / With sand-waves loving her brow" (lines 19-20), leaving Mabbie behind. Though I have not had a crush on someone, I know that I will never be rejected due to the color of my skin. Yet I cannot imagine what it would be like, but if I really paid attention to this poem, I can get an idea. I normally do not pay attention to the color of my skin, but after reading about how "chocolate" Mabbie is ignored in favor of someone more "lemon-hued," I begin to notice how skin color is perceived in ways I did not know before (line 19). I also get a taste of how a darker girl is forced to think about it because the outside world constantly reminds her of this fact. Though it is not a happy poem, I appreciate it not for "translating" itself into something I can relate to but for bringing to light a different experience so that I understand how nastily the world works for those less privileged than myself.

I receive the poem partially because I strive to be open-minded, but also because the poem tries to be intimate with me as a reader.[1]. Though the ballad is often told impersonally, the speaker calls Mabbie "our Mabbie" as her story comes to a close (line 18). This phrase acknowledges that there is an audience listening in on the story, and the reader is thus invested in what happens to Mabbie. The reader can then try to understand Mabbie, even if he or she many not relate to her. This makes sense since the ballad is a popular form, meaning of the people. Love is a popular topic among the common people and makes the ballad more relatable.

----

[1] This paragraph is perhaps the most interesting in the entire essay, from the standpoint of its description of how the poem works.

Not only is "the ballad of chocolate Mabbie" relatable but it is still relevant. A key characteristic of the ballad is repetition; its themes are repeated from generation to generation with some alterations. There is no date given for "the ballad of chocolate Mabbie" but based on the copyright date from the anthology it was taken from, it could have been written anytime from the forties to the seventies.[2]. Ultimately, however, the date would not matter because the poem's depiction of the racial gap in choosing a female mate could occur anytime from the past to the present. A 2011 film titled "Dark Girls" studies the phenomenon in more depth. It describes the rejection of darker skinned African American women by black men in favor of lighter-skinned or white women.

"Dark Girls" is basically the poem in documentary form. The only difference between the poem and the documentary is that the racism shown in the documentary is explicit. It is here that we see Mabbie's real life "chocolate companions." Several African American actresses are interviewed about their harsh experiences in the dating world. Viola Davis, for example, grew up "never seeing any examples on television or in film of anyone associated with beauty, softness, or kindness, or femininity that looked like me." They were teased, called racial epithets such as "tar baby" and told that "your skin is so dirty" by both white and black men (Dark Girls). There also seemed to be quite a few real-life Willie Boons. Random black men on the street were interviewed; one of them said, "They look funny beside me…I'd rather not date a dark skin woman. I'd rather light skin, pretty girl with long hair" (Dark Girls). Another black man on Facebook told an anonymous black girl that it was not his fault that lighter skinned women "simply looked prettier" (Dark Girls). None of these men may be aware of it, but there is a clear white supremacist ideal dictating their preferences. The average reader may also be unaware.

When a white person reads "the ballad of chocolate Mabbie," he or she will not find an experience but Mabbie's. The poem's language may be easy to understand, contrary to that of older poems Jarrell says modern readers often ignore, but its subject matter may be obscure due to the fact that African Americans are still considered a minority. Though a white reader may feel alienated at first, he or she should not discount the poem because it does everything it can to show how real and poignant the black girl's experience is. I was able to appreciate this poem's meaning as a result of its ballad form, despite the differences between Mabbie and I.

Works Cited

Brooks, Gwendolyn. Blacks. Chicago, Ill. (P.O. Box 19355, Chicago, Ill. 60619): David, 1987. Print.

---

[2] A Street in Bronzeville was published in 1945, so the poem was likely written early in the 1940s.

Dark Girls. Dir. Bill Duke. Perf. Stephanie A, Soren Baker, Joni Bovill, Viola
Davis, and Bill Johnson. Duke, 2011. Film.

Jarrell, Randall, and Brad Leithauser. "The Obscurity of the Poet." No Other
Book: Selected Essays. New York: HarperCollins, 1999. 3-18. Print.

HOPE MIRRLEES' PARIS: A POEM: THE FORGOTTEN WASTE LAND

BY AASHNA NAGPAL

Hope Mirrlees' Paris: A Poem not only antedates but also anticipates the canonical poem The Waste Land by Eliot. Yet it continues to be "Modernism's lost masterpiece" as Julia Briggs, the primary critic on the poem famously called it. The speaker of the poem describes the scenes she sees in the course of a day, a device central to Modernism's pivotal text- James Joyce's Ulysses and Virginia Woolf's Mrs Dalloway. The city of Paris comes alive through the poem as the speaker moves through it, while simultaneously moving temporally across Paris' rich historical phases. The poem's form and content follow along the lines of Modernism's urge to experiment with the written word.

The poem begins with a striking utterance: "I want a holophrase" (1). This can be a reference to the failings of language which Modernism was acutely aware of and constantly emphasized. There comes across an insufficiency of the existing language or it being beyond the scope of the speaker's knowledge. Julia Briggs, who is responsible for bringing Paris back from the dead, suggests this can also be a pun on "hollow phrase". The awareness of the futility of language becomes more apparent as the poem and the speaker move ahead. It moves on to naming the brands whose posters are on display in the underground railway station. "ZIG-ZAG/LION NOIR/CACAO BLOOKER"(3-5)- gives the effect of a movement so fast that it only allows the viewer/speaker no time to observe/elaborate anything beyond the name of the brand on the poster. One brand name thrown over another can be symbolic of the maddening frequency of stimuli in a metropolis where the second stimulus is thrown in the face before the first one could be grasped. It also indicates the exponential rate at which capitalism and consumerism was flourishing. Mirrlees only specifies what she really means by the three words in the 'Notes' she provides herself for the poem, something that T.S. Eliot does for Wasteland. The obscurity of the poem is thus intentional.

There is a sudden realization that the pace of the poem and the speaker has been fast- "I can't/ I must go slowly". An echo of this can be seen in Samuel Beckett's The Unnamable: "I can't go on. I shall go on". As if taking her own advice, the speaker goes slowly as indicated by the following words that are spaced and scattered. A few lines later, Mirlees writes, "Le départ pour Cythère"(29) which can be a reference to Charles Baudelaire's 'A Voyage to Cythera'. Several lines are filled with literary and art allusions, almost as if it were a catalogue, exactly like Eliot's 'The Waste Land'. The lines "Saunters the ancient rue Saint-Honoré/ Shabby and indifferent"(67-8), as Julia Briggs suggests, brings to mind the 'flâneur' or 'flâneuse' who saunters through the streets with a certain kind of indifference. The speaker's attention shifts between the overwhelming stimulus that the city lays out, while the speaker's intention of travelling through the railway and then on the streets is never explicitly mentioned. Here, though it is also the street 'rue Saint-Honoré' that saunters, as if the city itself was a flâneur and it moves as the speaker moves. The city seems more human than its inhabitants. Mirrlees writes, "Paris is a huge home-sick peasant, / He carries a thousand villages in his heart"(71-2). This can have several implications. The first being that Paris constantly lives in nostalgia, longing for what once was. In it everything exists in contradictions- the urban and the rural, peace and war, the dead living and the living dead. Mention of "Concorde" (17) itself shows contradictions co-existing since it was where the guillotine was placed during the Reign of Terror but is also the site of a peace agreement. The second being that it communicates an "ability to fracture the speaker's consciousness (only to restore its wholeness later)" (Parmar, 64). The poem abruptly shifts between English and French which implies that a single language would be completed inadequate to describe what the speaker is seeing as she goes on.

The movement in the poem happens both spatially and temporally. The metro line "NORD-SUD" (2), mentions of several stations, Place de la Concorde, specific street names of actual streets in Paris- all make the poem seem real. This is similar to how Joyce's routes in Dubliners can actually be traced through the city of Dublin. Temporally, Mirrlees evokes the French Revolution, times of Louis XVI while in the present a peace agreement is being signed. There is restlessness visible in how the speaker perceives time and is unable to situate the present in isolation from recent and distant past. The direction of both the spatial and temporal movement is undecided and non-linear, is subject to the whims of where the speaker wants to go next or where the streets and her thoughts take her. The poem is full of snippets of conversations that the speaker overhears and of fragments of thoughts, phrases and ideas. This mirrors the fragmented self of the modernist subject, which the speaker is very much so. Several sections of the poem are clusters of random images, creating the effect of an incessantly moving camera. These images and the thoughts may seem arbitrary but the manner in which they are arranged is in fact carefully crafted chain of thoughts written to look like a montage of images and a spontaneous stream of consciousness.

Mirrlees then shifts the focus to war and the mood of the poem changes for casual strolling to being preoccupied with death and violence. The speaker says, "The ghost of Père Lachaise/ Is walking the streets"(175-6) - the flaneuse isn't merely observing the tangible city but infusing in it a nightmarish vision of people coming back to life after being dead. Beyond the several advertisements, gardens filled with flowers there is an underlying awareness of the post-war metropolitan which becomes perceptible when Mirrlees writes, "The unities are smashed, and the stage is thick with corpses". World War I failed conspicuously to conform to any rules, let alone the unities of time, place and action required of classical tragedy. The loss of life, the scale of destruction, the extent of violence during war only intensifies the already existing inadequacy of language: "The coming to . . . . . . / Thick halting speech- the curse of vastness"(233-4). Half way through the poem, whatever the speaker sees and thinks defies language. The limits of language add to the sense of loss arising out of the destructions of war. There is so much to say that nothing is spoken. Right before this line in the poem appears: " Experience/ Very slowly/ Is forming up/ Into something beautiful-awful-huge" (229-232) which can also mean that the halting of the speech could be a result of the speaker being overwhelmed by the vastness of the city and its infinite details.

There is an apocalyptic image in the lines "Rain/ The Louvre is melting into mist"(264-5) where Louvre can be symbolic of the centre of the cultural capital of Paris. The reason behind the melting of the Louvre is not specified. Is it melting because the war tarnished the glory of French past? Can it be inferred from the melting of the Louvre that despite the concreteness of the metropolitan, nothing will endure the ravages of time? The line, "The Seine, the old egotist, meanders imperturbably towards the sea"(269) can be an echo of Eliot's Prufrock who meanders through the streets of London, then towards the sea in the climax of the poem. No matter how distinctly one might associate a river's or a person's identity to the city, the sea will always catch up. The sea humbles the city which was proud of its vastness. We can also interpret it as the speaker's attempt to see a flaneur in the river Seine itself since the word "meander" is chosen to describe its movement. The implication can be that the river, the streets, basically the city observes the people in it as much as a flaneur would observe the city.

Throughout the poem Mirrlees mentions several paintings that are displayed in museums in Paris to highlight the difference between art and reality: the stillness of the paintings contrasted with the relentless movement of the city, the permanency of the paintings with the transient lives of the city people. Yet, the actual city is only available in bits to the speaker so the only medium to make sense of it is seeing the city in painting. The line that follows- "Whatever happens, some day it will look beautiful"(286) condenses the speaker's stance on art, implying the beautification of the real as it is converted into art along with the ability of an artist to manipulate the world and the happenings. The incessant noise of the city is contrasted with the paintings that "hang in a quite gallery"(294). It is to be noted these paintings including "Manet's Massacres des Jours de Juin"(290) are depictions of violence which have been deprived of their goriness; the clamour, the tumult has been suppressed into a disturbing silence in the process of being painted. These lines bring out the failings of Realism since something or the other gets invariably lost in transition from the actual to art.

The dream-like images are acknowledged by the speaker when she says, "I wade knee-deep in dreams-"(310) which increase later in the poem: "The dreams have reached my waist"(377). This also shows that the speaker is conscious of certain aspects around her being figments of her imagination. There is no clarity as to which aspects since there is a deliberate blurring of the real and the imaginary, of the past and the present but the speaker is self-conscious about the role of her subconscious in her perception of the world. Dream-like images and visions induced in a trance were some of the basic tropes in Surrealism. The line, " Of citizens in masks and dominoes" echoes the motif of masks that recurs in the modernist poetry of Eliot, Pessoa and Baudelaire among others.

The speaker is finally able to get a bird's eye view of the city- "From the top of the floor of an old Hotel, / Tranced, / I gaze down at the narrow rue de Beaune"(319-21). There is a mention of Freud, whose work was a significant influence on the thinking of the twentieth century: "But behind the ramparts of the Louvre/ Freud has dredged the river and, grinning horribly, / waves his garbage in a glare of electricity"(414-6). Mirrlees uses typography, inserts bars of music within the poem, shows exceptional knowledge of Impressionist and Post-Impressionist paintings, evinces a cognisance of the aesthetics of Surrealism and ends her poem with a drawing of a constellation of Ursa Major.

The experimentation is very much deliberate, the intersections the poem has with other movements within Modernism are very apparent and its investment in the cultural history of the city is abundant. It can be insightful to ask why this poem remains at the margins of modernist poetry. Upon a critical look at the politics of canon-formation, at the fringes of art movements still remain unearthed masterpieces of literature.Let us saunter every now and then towards the outskirts of literary canons and discover art that sings with no one to hear it.

Bibliography

Mirrlees, Hope. Collected Poems Edited and Introduced by Sandeep Parmar. Manchester: Carcanet Press, 2011. Print.

ART HISTORY

BYZANTINE ART: A TIMELESS MARVEL

BY NEHASRI RAVISHENBAGAM

Byzantine Empire, also called the Eastern Roman Empire, was under Christian rule that thrived in the Middle Ages from 330 AD to 1453 AD. Byzantium (present-day Istanbul), as a Christian state, had Greek as its official language. The State practiced a Greco-Roman practice that was different from ancient Rome. As well as having impressive art, Literature, and culture, Byzantium also served as a military buffer between Asia and Europe. Despite the collapse of the Western part of Rome (ruled from Rome) in 476 AD, the Eastern Part (ruled from Byzantium) stood strong for more than 1000 years. With the Western Empire's fall, thousands of Greek and Roman artists and Craftsmen marched towards Byzantium and contributed to a new art style called Byzantine art.

What is a Byzantine Art?

The Byzantine Empire was home to a wide range of western art forms including sculptures, mosaics, and paintings that are still revered today. As this glittering period of Medival Art existed over a millennium, it got categorized into three phases-Early Byzantine Era (330-730), Middle Byzantine Era (843-1204), and Later Byzantine Era (1261-1453).

Mosaic of "The Virgin and the child" in Hagia Sophia, Istanbul

Traditionally, Byzantine art comprised of Christian Greek images and icons that ultimately flourished into Orthodox Christianity. Mostly, the icons of Christ, the Virgin Mary, and scenes from the Bible were used, to decorate Churches and even private homes all over the Mediterranean to get hold of the figure's holy presence. Even Churches encouraged the art techniques as they brought fresh ideas to the plate, such as the domed roofs in churches to make them seem aesthetically pleasing with shimmering mosaic works.

The Byzantine artists adorned their works with bright stones, extravagant gold mosaics, murals, precious metals, wall paintings, ivory carvings, and frescoes. They aimed to create exaggerated and idealized images to symbolize what they believed existed in a human's soul. The artists aspired to render the audience with an experience of a spiritual realm.

Mosaics

With their Biblical themes, Mosaics deserve special mention in the history of Byzantine art. From the 6th century to the end of the Byzantine Empire in the 15th century, the Mosaics were an extremely popular form of expression. Byzantine artists, unlike the Romans, made Mosaic art with thousands of small pieces of glass, ceramics, and stones, called the Tesserae. The realistic depictions of floating figures with golden Tesserae in the Mosaics inspire a sense of wonder and admiration for the Church. In addition, the Byzantine Mosaic works also stood unique by incorporating lavish materials in their works-gold and silver leaves and precious stones that leave a sparkling effect.

A Byzantine Mosaic in Ravenna, Italy

Major surviving proofs of Byzantine art and architecture

1. Hagia Sophia

Interiors of Hagia Sophia, Istanbul

The Byzantine art reached its zenith with the Byzantine Emperor, Justinian I (527-565). A notable monument of his, Hagia Sophia, in present-day Istanbul is the living evidence of the glorious Byzantine art form. With numerous windows, soaring minarets, bright-colored famous Mosaics, and glittering gold highlights, the architectural style of Hagia Sophia is adored by millions today. Although it had some of the finest Mosaics during its initial construction stage, it has suffered more than one destruction and has undergone several reconstructions throughout the centuries.

Also known as the Church of Holy wisdom, it required around 10,000 artists to decorate the interiors during, Justinian I's reign. Originally the Hagia Sophia was built as a Christian Orthodox church that served a purpose for centuries. Upon the Ottoman conquest in 1453, Hagia Sophia was transformed into a mosque. With time, many Byzantine artworks got destroyed, but Ravenna in Italy helps one rediscover some of the best evidences of this period.

Basilica di San Vitale

The Church of San Vitale in Ravenna is a hotspot today with numerous mosaics that depict several historical figures of its time and much more. It is also considered a masterpiece of Byzantine architecture with its celebrated murals of Christian icons that decorate the interiors. Built in an octagonal shape, the Church especially combines the Roman architectural style-The dome, stepped towers, and the shape of doors with Byzantine style-narrow bricks, capitals, and a polygonal apse. The most important asset the place holds is the mosaic of Emperor Justinian I.

Even today, the Byzantine Empire still has a profound influence on many western states, including Russia and Europe, especially in religion, architecture, art, and law. Though the Byzantine Iconoclasm destroyed many early artworks due to its condemnation of religious icons and images, its timeless art and architecture are still cherished by millions today. Due to this, most Byzantine mosaics that survived were made between the 10th and 12th centuries as the previous ones faced damages.

Mosaic of Justinian I in San Vitale, Ravenna, Italy

NIGERIAN NOK CIVILIZATION

BY EDITA BOJANAC DELCARO

Back in the 1940s, when the miners superficially excavated tin in Nigeria, surprisingly beautiful terracotta figures, stone tools, and other finds appeared on the plain of Jos. The Nok civilization, also called Nok figurine culture, was a great discovery for the world as one of the earliest fully developed cultures of the Iron Age.

The civilization, famous for their pottery, flourished in the second half of the first millennium BC – from around 500 BC to 200 CE in southern West Africa (modern-day Nigeria), according to radiocarbon data off charcoal found among the furnaces. Within decorative terracotta and pottery, tools and weapons with iron blades were also discovered, with the evidence of melting the iron (iron slag and furnace remains).

In the Taruga village (55 km southeast of Abuja) archaeologists have also found the iron-smelting furnaces, but the Nok people have also known and used stone and metal tools, being one of the few that transitioned from stone tools straight to iron, skipping the Bronze Age.

The remains of the grindstone confirm that grain was grown, and the abundance of finely ground quartz grains, pierced with tiny iron needles so that it could be guided to the thread are telling us that they loved to adorn themselves.

The Nok civilization was a culture with a very developed sense of aesthetics, artists created shapes by lowering balls of moist clay, and this is repeated on bracelets and necklaces as well. The figures are found mostly in fragments, buried under eight meters of sand – representing humans, elephants, monkeys, snakes, and other animals.

Figures of people could be about 1.40 meters high – with expressive triangular eyes pierced in the middle, as well as skillfully crafted hairstyles, buns, or braids. They ran strings of beads or pearls through their hair, while their faces expressed a whole range of emotions, from anger, anxiety, resentment, which often seemed excessive.

Unlike human forms, animal figures are more restrained and realistic. The explanation for the distorted depictions of human figures may be found in the fact that many West African societies lived in fear of sorcery.

Today we know that Nok was the first sub-Saharan culture in perfecting the iron-smelting, covering some 78,000 square kilometers. There are some regional differences in the types of tools and pottery made. However, further details from their everyday life, population, economy, and social structure remain relatively unknown.

Likewise many other Iron Age cultures, the Nok people inflicted the greatest damage on themselves, overexploiting the natural resources – large areas were simply stripped of deforestation due to the demand for the fuel needed for smelting, resulting in dryland prone to erosion. This advanced culture disappeared at the end of the first millennium BC, leaving their legacy hard to determine.

Fast checking files

1. The Nok civilization was a great discovery for the world as one of the earliest fully developed culture of the Iron Age.

The Nok Culture | National Geographic Society

2. The civilization, famous for their pottery, flourished in the second half of the first millennium BC.

The Nok Culture | National Geographic Society

3. Today we know that Nok was the first sub-Saharan culture in perfecting the iron-smelting,

Nok Culture - World History Encyclopedia

4. The figures are found mostly in fragments, buried under eight meters of sand

Nok Culture - World History Encyclopedia

5. The Nok civilization, also called Nok figurine culture, was a great discovery for the world as one of the earliest fully developed culture of the Iron Age.
Nok culture | Iron Age culture | Britannica
6. However, further details from their everyday life,population, economy, and social structure remain a mystery.
Nok - Art & Life in Africa - The University of Iowa Stanley Museum of Art (uiowa.edu)

Sources:

The Nok Culture | National Geographic Society

Nok Culture - World History Encyclopedia

The Nok: People & Culture | Study.com

Nok culture | Iron Age culture | Britannica

Nok - Art & Life in Africa - The University of Iowa Stanley Museum of Art (uiowa.edu)

Nok civilisation - Think Africa

Restitution of a cultural property of the Nok civilization (unesco.org)

OTHER ARTICLES

A SYSTEM OF PHRENOLOGY AND THE POWER OF BEING WRONG

BY BILYANA HADZHIKYANOVA

George Combe (1788-1858), famous as the most prominent phrenologist, was a seeker and an advocate of truth. He played a dual role in psychology as a leading British phrenologist, natural philosopher and an author of the best-selling book The Constitution of Man, which laid out the physical, psychological and moral laws governing human nature. Combe promoted a concept of human nature that reflected the overriding importance of self-improvement and moral conviction and gave a more secular view of man's place in the universe.

When describing George Combe, his mental healthcare reformer Sir James Coxe would pave his being with "detestation of all shams, a craving for truth, and a love of justice."

His phrenological research, though, will be the one to teach humanity that even the most prolific truth seekers can sometimes be terribly wrong, which can still turn out incredibly beneficial to society.

To grasp the importance of George Combe's controversial contribution, we will have to shed some light on the phenomenon named phrenology. Its initial inventor was the physician Franz Joseph Gall (1758-1828) who came up with his theory when he noticed that his medical classmates who did well on exams tended to have 'large, prominent eyes'. He tried to establish a connection between the functions of the brain and its regions by studying the skulls of people who stood out sharply with their mental abilities. This inspired him to start gathering anecdotal evidence and later on examined the skulls of famous writers, poets, politicians as well as some cases of lunatics and criminals.

Gall believed the measurements of the human skull can determine personality traits, talent, and mental abilities, which can be categorized and localized into separate regions called brain organs. Combe would later rename these categories and further divide them into more areas corresponding to a faculty of the human mind such as: caution, benevolence, memory, perception of time, struggle, and perception of form.

Regardless of the mass fascination with George's ideas among the Victorian community, phrenology was never accepted as scientifically viable. However, some of its main pillars paved the way for the development of a real scientific field - neurobiology. For example, some the original insights into how different areas of the brain are associated with different functions were important in shaping a new understanding of how the brain works.

The greatest contribution of Phrenology to medicine is its aroused interest in the scientific community to understand the human mind and how it relates to the brain. Although debunked by advances in neuroscience, some ideas put forward by phrenologists have been confirmed. Modern brain imaging has allowed scientists to localize functions in the brain. The faculty of verbal memory is close to the areas of Broca and Wernicke, which are now known as important areas for speech. In spite of the scientific inconsistency, phrenology is indirectly used to teach research on morphology and physiology on the nervous system and stimulation of development on anthropometry and anthropology.

The excitement around phrenology faded away already in the 20th century. The science of the structure of the skull was replaced by psychology and psychoanalysis. The study is not of external signs, but of the internal, mental state. In a sense, phrenology was the preparatory stage that made the advent of psychoanalysis possible. George Combe himself believed to have unveiled some of the secrets of human nature and was disappointed by the way his ideas were predominantly treated:

"It is mischievous to the community at large to throw obstacles in the way of the study of [phrenology], and it is unjust to those who have opened it up to the public's eye, to misrepresent their success. Every general announcement, that Phrenology is not to be trusted to, is a reason assigned for not studying it, and is a positive condemnation of those who maintain that it is founded in nature. In every other science, the testimony of those, who have cultivated it most, is, ceteris paribus, allowed to have most weight; and I have never been able to see, why this rule should be reversed in the case of Phrenology.'

Combe is the most influential figure behind phrenology's survival and popularisation in the English-speaking world. Even though phrenology never received scientific approval, he remains in history as the most prolific author of phrenological works. A lawyer by education who did not even get to study medicine, his findings and extraordinary life illustrate how perseverance could influence and completely change lives. It also portrayed how ideas based on the willingness to believe in them rather than scientifically proven facts should be handled with special attention as at any point, one could be tremendously wrong.

POETRY

OH RAIN

BY TRUPTI REKHA DASMAHAPATRA

Oh rain!
We are wondering
From where you came,
You heal everyone's pain
Without you all are insane.

Oh rain,
All are sad when you are not gained,
Farmers await, plants look forward
When you are not there, all are vein.

Oh rain,
Everyone gets scared
With thunder when you come,
We bother
When you show your rude appearance.

Oh rain,
We are blessed
With heavenly touch when you come,
Make us wet and give us a cool sigh
World is full of water,
Still, we look forward your arrival.

Oh rain,
You make this world green,
Make all of us happy and give us food
You give us relaxed breath,
When we spend summer.

Oh rain,
Birds cripples when you come,
Frogs sing and peacocks dance

Morning sun welcomes you with dimmed ray,
Children thank you for escaping from school.

Oh rain,
You didn't realize
In Everyone's face you bring smile,
Farmers relax when you pour lots of drops
Flowers blossom and fishes swim.

Oh rain,
We become happy
With rainbow when you come,
We are mentally healed
When we get wet with your drops.

Oh rain,
You are the cause of billions of smiles,
Reason of everyone's food and sigh
You are the cause of Everyone's tiny happiness,
You are the best creation of God.

THE WHY OF LIFE

BY PEACE POON

The Why Of Life is for those who inspire us:

Our families.
Our friends.
Our partners.

The ones who make us feel heard;
The ones who love us for who we are.

They're not fond of rules;
And they have no respect for those who hurt us.

We can:
Call them,
Invite them,
Bond or bicker with them.

About the only thing we can't do is ignore them,
Because they change us.
They make us a better version of ourselves each day.

While some may see them as complete strangers,
We see companions;
Because those who inspire others to do what they love--
Inspire us to do what we love.

And together,
We may find--

The Why Of Life.

INSOMNIA

BY AASHNA NAGPAL

I don't know if the crows
Have disappeared from where I live
Or if I have stopped looking
Outside the window.

I undress myself
A rotten fruit being peeled,
I discard myself onto the bed.

Rusty brick walls are lined with
Withered white lilies chipping off
Waiting to be blown away.

The song that the watchman sings
To keep himself awake puts me to sleep.
I hear myself snore.

Faces are places with one way ticket,
The gypsy tongue argues
With itself all night.

Ragged curtain's flapping-
The background music of
My dreams, like the fading lullaby
Streaming through a fading street.

Someone's ringing the bell
At someone's door to tell something
That they wouldn't want to hear.

I can sleep only with my right knee
Pressing against my stomach

While the fan is faintish,
The tap drooling on the sink.

Twisted faces, low-pitched screams
Twitching hands, blackness, blankness
The hourglass face, horizontal time.

Where does the dust go
When there are no corners?

CHANGE

BY MICHAEL STROUP

The world we live in grows oh so cold

I've witnessed good and bad

But in the end, it's the same when we grow old.

This world prides itself on its monetary gain

And all that does is cause the ones we love so much pain

Where did the times go when we looked out for one another?

Oh, that's right we left it to rot inside our tarnished gutters.

We no longer offer an open hand

We just stand around and laugh as others are pushed into the sand.

We walk the walk and we talk the talk

But would you be there to help instead of just to gawk

The sad reality is no you wouldn't

The first thing most of us would do is pull out our phones, even when we know we shouldn't.

In the day and age where talking to one another has died

Maybe now is the time that we will swallow our pride.

To make a change in time so dark

How could you not care about another person, unless of course, you have no heart?

The good we could bring to the world knows no bounds

And to be frank it's not as hard as it sounds.

All we need to do is open our eyes to see the truth

Because the future rests upon our youth.

Teach your children respect for the earth

Respect for the place where we all were birthed

Change will not happen overnight

But just because of that doesn't me we shouldn't fight

Fight for a better future, fight for a greater cause, fight for what is right

Because our time here in this world is finite

But if we work together we can finally end this blight

And when our time here is done

Maybe just maybe my children can play in the sun

So listen and listen close, for these words I tell are true.

Change starts with me, with us, change starts with you. -MJS

SHORT STORY

A FLABBERGASTED DREAM

BY TRUPTI REKHA DASMAHAPATRA

It was 3.00 am. Zac was sweating a lot. He got up from his deep sleep and sat for some time to convince himself that it was a dream not a reality. The dream didn't allow him to get back to sleep again and he wanted to smoke heading towards the balcony. After having a cigarette in his mouth, he tried to recollect the incident that occurred in his dream. The chill breeze of the early morning in the balcony tried to take him to comfort zone but he didn't give up pondering to recollect the dream incident. He could visualize that someone was telling him something but he couldn't get the clear picture of the person and the wordings. Three cigarettes were burnt up to ashes without having any cogent inference. Suddenly he heard a voice, "what are you doing there at this moment?" It was his mom's voice which brought him back to the world of reality again.

While going to the office he picked up Christina and dropped her at her office in order to move ahead to his workplace. But the dream incident of last night didn't allow him to concentrate on his work. He took a long break and sat for sometime in a remote place with a packet of cigarettes. As he tried to recollect the dream incident, his heart beat went faster and he felt his blood flow in his body was faster than the speed of light. He went into the contemplation digging a lot about his dream. He could visualize again someone was telling him something. He was struggling a lot to go beyond this level to know what was happening in his dream but the speed of his heartbeat was increasing and he was sweating a lot at that moment. The call from Christina broke his contemplation and instructed him to pick her up from the office while returning. He became so crazy as he could not draw the clear picture of the incident that happened in his dream and decided to share this with Christina. After picking her up from her office, he drove to a coffee shop to have some coffee which was a great surprise for Christina. It had been almost 10 years of their relationship, Zac never cared to take her to a café to have coffee together. She was so happy that Zac took her to a special place to spend some time with her and she could not express her feelings with excitement. With mixed feelings of love and blush, she asked, "what do you prefer to have, cappuccino?" But she received no response from Zac and realized that he was in some other tension. She took his hand and tried to rub his palm with love to make him relaxed. Before she asked Zac regarding the cause of his tautness, Zac started explaining the situations he went through since the past three days. At the end of the conversation, Christina burst out laughing when she came to know that there was an unknown reason for his tautness. Zac shouted at her publicly without controlling his temper and left that place. Christina's surprise became a bad experience that day.

Before Zac went to bed at night, he decided to avoid thinking more about that dream incident. He tried to relax himself and slept well. A mild sound of train horn broke his sleep; as he decided to sleep well without thinking anything, he tried to block his two ears with his palms so as not to get disturbed but he couldn't sleep. The volume of the train horn increased and he got up. He walked towards the window to look outside. He could see the train rushing in a high speed on a body and that body split into multiple pieces. "Oh my God!" screeching he ran down to see who it was. As soon as he opened his eyes, he could find himself in his bed room lying on the bed. He got up from bed and his body was full of sweat. He relaxed himself with a long breath saying, "Thank God; it was a dream". He was feeling tired and worried as strange things were happening with him and it was very hard to explain his situation to anyone. He tried to go to sleep once again and slept well. Next day morning he went to take a bath and stood under the shower. He tried to recollect the dream and could view a vague picture of an old lady telling him the story and his dream rerouted to a train which was rushed towards the south with a loud sound of horn. Again he could view the vague picture of a dead body on the railway track cut into pieces after the train had passed. All of sudden he felt the chilled water drops falling on his head and body and he realized that he was having shower. From the past few days the dream incidents were bothering him a lot. He was wondering, **who was telling the story? And whose story was it anyway? The words of that old lady fluttered and flew away in the wind.** He was trying to force himself to visualize the clear picture of different incidents he had dreamt and how it was connected with his life. In fact, he was not sure if these incidents were connected with his life or not.

His boss Peter called him to his cabin and gave him shocking news. Zac had to move abroad to present the project they were working on for the prolonged period. Peter encouraged Zac to present the project on behalf of the company. Zac could not believe it as he did not expect the news at this time. Anyway, he had come out from the dream incidents and was ready to move thinking about the pleasure of his trip of 6 months. He called Christina and gave the good news but it was not good for her. Zac was going to stay away from her for six months. She found it so hard to convince herself to be away from him. Zac was quite practical and excited as well to move abroad but Christina was neither happy nor able to express her feelings to Zac. She wanted Zac to be happy and that's the reason she decided to keep quiet without expressing her feelings to him. Finally the moment arrived when Zac had to leave his native place for a few months and Christina started counting the days when Zac would come back.

In the new place, the awesome sights and intelligent people took all the attention of Zac and kept him away from his family including Christina. Gradually, Zac involved himself completely in this new city and new surroundings working on his project, which resulted in the less frequencies of having contact with his family and Christina. He met his colleague Diana in the new office and worked hand in hand with her and fell in love in a few days. He started enjoying and spending more time with Diana forgetting Christina. Three months passed and he felt as if he had come to this place very recently. The time passed and the project got over but his serious love story started from then. He was not ready to come back to India leaving Diana. Next day he explained his situation and expressed his feelings of love to Diana. They decided to get married and returned to India.

Christina was very excited as the time for Zac being in was over and he will be back to India in a few days. She prepared herself very well to welcome him back to India with all surprises and started imagining the moment when she would meet Zac in the airport. At last, the moment came. Zac's mom, Christina and Christina's grandmother reached the airport to welcome Zac back home. The arrival announcement of the flight made the heartbeat of Christina faster and she started blushing imagining the arrival of Zac from far away. In the meanwhile, she could see Zac was coming up holding someone's hand. "Whose hand is this?" she whispered to herself. It was a girl whose company made Zac smile and happy. She had never seen Zac smiling from the core of his heart when he was with her. The sounds from the surroundings were blurred to her and she was stunned for a few minutes. She was trying to manage herself by hiding her feelings and emotions. Zac's mom and Christina's grandmother were also shocked and stood speechless seeing Diana with Zac. Without reacting, Zac introduced Diana with everyone saying, "Meet my wife Diana". Zac's mother and Christina's grandmother became speechless and stared at Christina. Managing herself and her feelings wisely, Christina smiled at both Diana and Zac and welcomed them in a formal way. She could notice Zac was not able to look at her eyes and tried avoiding direct eye contact. Hiding all her feelings and anxiety she managed herself very well in front of Zac and Diana.

At night, Diana slept well as she was very tired but Zac did not get proper sleep. He could hide the feelings he had for Christina from Diana but not from himself. His all the old memories didn't let him sleep and forced him to think about Christina. All the old days' journey and the time that spent with her were really golden memories he felt. He came out from the room and started walking towards Christina's house. He saw her grandmother sitting in a rocking chair and cradling herself in the upstairs. He went up and started asking a lot of questions about Christina. Grandmother started telling all the incidents that happened within these six months. How Christina denied all the proposals for her marriage and how she was looking at Zac's photo all the time. Christina never spent a single moment without Zac's memory. She fought with her friends and colleagues because they were teasing her saying Zac had got married to someone else there. She had confidence in Zac more than herself. "If she did not tell you anything in the airport, that doesn't mean she has forgiven you", said grandmother dropping two drops of tears from her eyes. "You have not only hurt her, but hurt me and your mom. It's your wish to choose your partner but at least you could have informed us about your marriage" said grandmother in a sad voice.

Zac was realizing as if he had listened those words previously whatever grandmother was telling him at that moment. His ears were getting blocked but he tried to rob his ears in order to listen those words properly. Again, he could hear the train sound in increasing volume and he got up from the chair towards the window without listening to grandmother's words. "Ops dammit, I have seen this scene somewhere", he told himself. As soon as he looked through the window, he could see the train rushing on a body and that body turned into several pieces. He ran downstairs and looked for Christina. Christina was not there in her bedroom. Zac rushed toward the train track and was stunned. It was Christina's body which he was dreaming of several times six months back. "Oh my God!" he could not control his emotions and knelt down there. He started screaming, "Christina please forgive me. I have done wrong with you. I love you so much but I don't know why I have chosen Diana". He wished to hug her but there were several parts of her body lying down here and there. Zac was not sure if he could survive for a long time with the burden of Christina's death...

ACROSS THE WAY

BY MADISON LIPSKY

My toes crinkle up in the crunchy sand as if to grasp its home before it is washed away forever. Lee Ann Womack would be proud as I do feel small while I stand beside the North Atlantic. I wonder what could be beyond my eye line, beyond the vast horizon.

Maybe across the wide sea of undiscovered waters is a little boy who also has sand clutched beneath his preadolescent toes. His name is James. James has pasty, freckly skin and big pale blue eyes that light up the night sky. He is his parents' pride and joy, along with his four other siblings that share the same distinct physical characteristics. He is merely seven years old who has been accustomed to the beautiful land of Ireland throughout his life. He stands on the Ireland coast, big blue waves, as blue as his eyes, stretch out in front of him, and captivating lands of green reside alongside him. As he stares into the mysterious ocean, he wonders what the world consists of as he knows nothing else but his Irish decent.

Maybe across the Ocean is a faithful mother who lives in Liberia. Her name is Adah, which means a beautiful ornament, originating from the Hebrew language. She is indeed beautiful, but she prefers her strength over her beauty. Her upper arm muscles are outlined within her dark complexion. Her black braided hair falls down her back and she wears a brightly colored dress that flows gracefully, allowing moving shadows to dance on her knees. She stands on the Coast of Western Africa in hopes that one day soon her two daughters will have the same freedom and rights as a woman who lives across the way.

It is possible that slightly below from where I stand is a young couple, deeply in love, dancing to music on the Venezuela beaches. His hands are gently cradling her hips, swaying to the sound of the drums while twinkling lights shine above their unwavering heads. As they look deep into each other's eyes they forget that there is no other place in the world but right where they are.

Through the rough waters and calm seas, miles, and miles away from where I stand there may be an old man who resides on the coast of Portugal. His name is Filipe, and he is an incredibly gifted artist. He once traveled around the world painting landscapes of each place he visited. But now he seldom travels, instead he paints his deceased wife and waits until the day he will be reunited with her once more. His hair is as grey as the sky was on the day which his beloved passed. His veiny hands shake with agony from all the years of cradling his paintbrush but that does not stop him from painting a distinctively detailed portrait of his wife's hazel eyes. He is undeniably well-traveled but his favorite place in the world is Mendoza, Argentina. This is where he met his wife back in 1983. They fell in love instantly and a few years later they had their first and only child.

She could live in Spain, far across from where I stand. Her name is Camila, named after her beloved mother. She was born in Argentina, raised in Portugal, and now lives on the coast of Spain as an elementary school teacher. Her true passion is teaching and paving the way for the children of our future. She is short and petite, with black curly hair that resembles her energetic personality. She has bright almond-shaped eyes, similar to the ones in her father's paintings. She frequently considers moving to the city of Sydney, Australia to try her hand in surfing, while still pursuing her gift of teaching. She has her whole life ahead of her.

Maybe, young James will grow old one day and meet the love of his life as he is backpacking through Israel. She will be bold and courageous. She will be a rare woman, one who does whatever she wants without the approval or acceptance of others. She will light up James's world in an instant and will break through all of his comfort zones, allowing him to grow through her presence. Her name will be Maria. Maria will have an alluring smile and a heart-shaped birthmark aligned on her collarbone. She will be the daughter of a young couple who fell in love on a Venezuela beach.

If Camila finds herself in the extraordinary country of Australia, she will meet two sisters who were born and raised on the coast of Liberia. They will become close friends and will share with Camila the story about how their mother moved them across the world for hopes of a better life as independent women. Their names will be Mandisa and Lerato and like their mother, they will be exceptionally beautiful, but most importantly, they will be strong. They both will have a surprising knack for surfing and will train Camila to become as skilled at conquering the ocean as they are.

I stand on the east coast shore of Maryland, my toes still clutching the soggy sand. I feel so small yet so free. I do not know if these people exist, but I am sure of these places. It is only a matter of time before I go across the way and find out for myself exactly who and what the world has to offer.

A STORY ABOUT MR CAPITALISM AND HIS TWO HOSTAGES – MR SCIENCE AND MR MEDIA

BY KARLO TASLER

Mr Capitalism woke up sweaty in his big mansion. He sat on the edge of his bed and stared anxiously at a luxurious golden chandelier. His lips formed the shape of smile, but his clenched teeth, wrinkles on his forehead, and exposed veins on his neck indicated it was not a smile but rather an expression of suffering. He took medicine from the bedside table and swallowed it without water.

"Ok, I am alright!" he said when he looked at himself in the mirror. He smoothed down his hair to one side and dressed up in the silver suit.

It was raining when he got out of the mansion in a huge garden. He put a baseball cap on his head to protect himself from rain and went towards the end of the garden where a laboratory was based.

He opened the laboratory door and saw Mr Science giving the final check to his new vaccine. Mr Science's face seemed happy, even though his head was swapped with his right knee. Namely, unlike other people, Mr Science had a superpower to swap different body parts with each other. For example, he could take his eyes off and swap them with his left arm to change the perspective and make his discoveries more relevant. Sometimes he would swap his entire face with his foot to see if the face masks work against viruses at the level of increased density. However, if he missed just one part of his body, he would be utterly dysfunctional. Science needed all of his body parts because if he lost one, the full perspective would be gone. One body part made sense for another one. Only as a whole Science could work.

"Oh, that is you," Science said gruntingly and put his head with black thick hair back on his shoulder when Capitalism entered the laboratory.

Now with his body in place, Science's satisfied face turned worried. He put the vaccine in the pocket of his white scrub.

"I need you, Science," Capitalism said as he closed the door behind himself.

"What do you need me for this time?" Science asked and crossed his arms as he had something to defend.

"What do you mean what for?" Capitalism was confused. "For money, of course!"

"I am sorry, but I can't leave my laboratory," Science said as a cramp appeared on his cheek.

"I need you to go with me," Capitalism said and took off the cap from his head.

"I am sorry, I have some work to do to make the world a safer place," Science said, turned his back to Capitalism and kept working.

Capitalism got angry. He took a plastic bag from his back pocket, approached Science from the back and put the bag onto Science's head.

"Heeelp!" Science screamed, but before he had a chance to defend, he was already unconscious.

"Look what you did to yourself now," Capitalism said as he started dragging Science towards the exit.

He opened the door single-handedly and got Science out of the laboratory. He put him in a shed next to the laboratory, tied his arms around the pillar with a rope and took the bag off his head.

"Arrrghhh," Science shouted when Capitalism watered him with the hose.

"Leave me alone, I can't help you," Science said as he got conscious, trying to cut the rope with quick movements.

"You will damage your scrub if you keep doing this."

"Leave me alone," Science repeated.

"If you are not willing to cooperate, I will need to get violent, you know that."

"Heeelp," Science started shouting.

"I will need this," Capitalism said as he grabbed Science by his left arm.

"No!" Science said when he managed to get his hand out of Capitalism's grip. "What are you doing?"

"I need your left arm!"

"You can't have my left arm," Science said. "The Left arm is dysfunctional without the rest of my body. And the rest of the body is dysfunctional without the left arm. I am Science, I only function as a whole."

"I need only your left arm, the one that says lockdown is here to prevent the spread of the virus."

"You can't have it!" Science again managed to shook Capitalism off. "Left arm, which says lockdown is here to stop the spread of the virus, does not work without the right arm, which says lockdown will only be useful for vulnerable people until the vaccine has been created and that lockdown would create major psychophysical disorders for the rest of the population."

"Oh, shut up. I don't need your right arm, it's useless. I have billions of PCR tests ready to sell," Capitalism said. "I can't sell all of them without a global lockdown. PCR tests are the ticket for freedom," Capitalism said and ripped off Science's left arm.

Science shut down.

Capitalism closed the shed's door and left Science in the dark, with only a tiny gap between the door and floor for air to flow into the shed.

Capitalism started shaking, sweat drops burst out of his skin. He took medicine from his suit pocket and swallowed it while holding Science's arm in his other hand.

"I am alright," he consoled himself as he swept sweat from his forehead and went to another shed, distant five meters away from the first one.

"Media!" Capitalism shouted when he opened the door. "Wake up!"

"Oh, shit," Mr Media muttered when he opened his eyes while lying on the wooden floor curled up in a ball.

Media was dressed in an old, scratched shirt with a diamond pattern. He had spectacles with the left glass broken.

"Publish this," Capitalism said when he threw Science's left arm on the floor next to Media.

"No!" Media said quietly as he adjusted his spectacles. "You know I can't publish Science's left arm, which says lockdown is here to stop the spread of the virus, without the right arm, which says lockdown will only be useful for vulnerable people until the vaccine has been created and that lockdown would create major psychophysical disorders for the rest of the population. I need both arms for a holistic approach."

"Oh, you and fucking Science, always the same story," Capitalism got angry. "Could you please for once remember who is funding you?"

"It is you who is funding me," Media said in a contrite tone.

"That is right, my friend," Capitalism smoothed his tone as well. "You know that with a holistic approach to the situation I can't make all the profit. Only with the single perspective we can make all the profit, and we both can keep running. Only with a single perspective, we can make people buy all those PCR tests as a ticket for freedom. You do know how I work and how I finance you."

"I don't want that anymore!" Media shouted. "I want to get out of it, I want to offer people the full perspective, I want to get back to the essence of journalist work, I want to inform people."

"It is too late for that, my friend. There is no you without me, don't you remember?" Capitalism said and pointed on the Science's left arm. "Now, publish it."

"I am sorry, but I am opting out," Media said while ignoring the arm.

"Is that right?" Capitalism asked apologetically before he stamped on Media's fingers.

"Heeelp," Media screamed in pain.

"There is nobody to help you," Capitalism said and put more pressure.

"Heeeelp!" Media screamed again.

"I am the only one who can help you," Capitalism said. "And you can also help me. We have been working beautifully for so long. Why are you ruing it now?"

"I have been your hostage, and you have been exploiting me," Media said.

"Ohh," Capitalism realised and lifted his foot from Media's hand. "Media... Let's not pretend, you are obsessed with me. I didn't invite you here in the first place, you came here voluntarily. Just as Science did."

"That is because you told me you had noble things to share, and that was a lie. You tricked me."

"I didn't trick you. I just gave you one side of the story that we both needed to make a narrative we needed."

"I want out of that!"

"It is too late for that, my friend," Capitalism said and pointed on the Science's left arm. "We have become one. I can't live without you, you can't live without me."

Media didn't say anything, just bent his neck in misery.

"Now publish it," Capitalism pushed Science's left arm closer to Media with his leg.

Media took the arm and published it.

Contact us

You can contact Hermes Magazine in these ways.

Email:
Hermesmagazinelondon@yahoo.com

LinkedIn:
www.linkedin.com/company/hermesmagazine

Website:
www.hermesmagazine.yolasite.com